Multiplying and dividing 5–6

Author: Lynn Huggins-Cooper
Illustrators: Emma Holt and Chris McGhie

How to use this book

Look out for these features!

IN THE ACTIVITIES

The parents' notes at the top of each activity will give you:
► a simple explanation about what your child is learning
► an idea of how you can work with your child on the activity.

This small page number guides you to the back of the book, where you will find further ideas for help.

These magic stars provide useful facts and helpful hints!

AT THE BACK OF THE BOOK

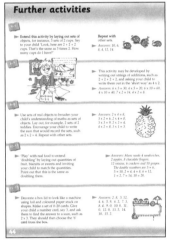

Every activity has a section for parents containing:
► further explanations about what the activity teaches
► games that can be easily recreated at home
► questions to ask your child to encourage their learning
► tips on varying the activity if it seems too easy or too difficult for your child.

You will also find the answers at the back of the book.

HELPING YOUR CHILD AS THEY USE THIS BOOK

Why not try starting at the beginning of the book and work through it? Your child should only attempt one activity at a time. Remember, it is best to learn little and often when we are feeling wide awake!

EQUIPMENT YOUR CHILD WILL NEED

► a pencil for writing
► an eraser for correcting mistakes
► coloured pencils for drawing and colouring in.

You might also like to have ready some spare paper and some collections of objects (for instance, small toys, Lego bricks, buttons...) for some of the activities.

Contents

Adding over and over

Look at these long sums.
There is a way to make them easier using 'x'.

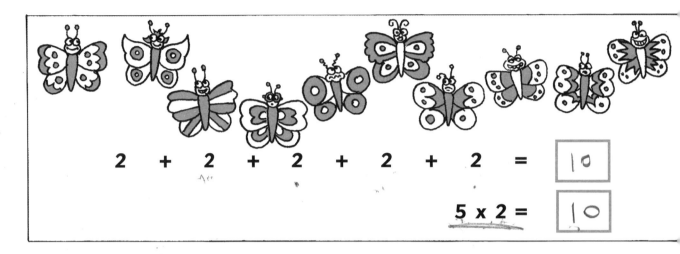

2 + 2 + 2 + 2 + 2 = $\boxed{10}$

5 x 2 = $\boxed{10}$

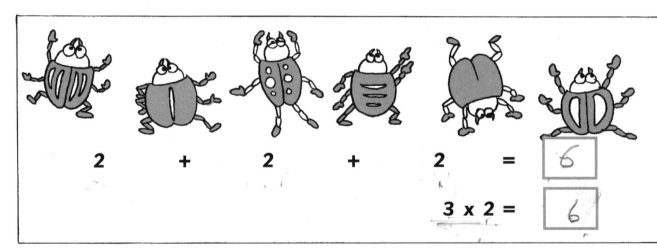

2 + 2 + 2 = $\boxed{6}$

3 x 2 = $\boxed{6}$

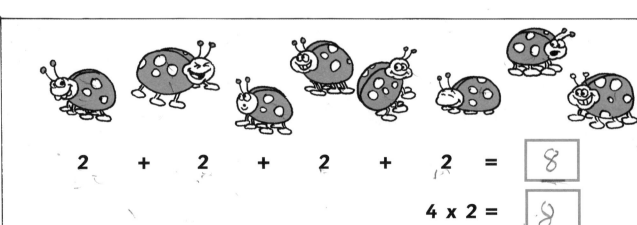

2 + 2 + 2 + 2 = $\boxed{8}$

4 x 2 = $\boxed{8}$

This activity introduces multiplication as 'repeated addition'.

Help your child to complete both the addition and multiplication sums, using their fingers if necessary.

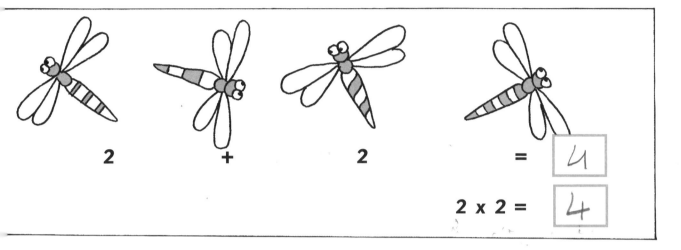

2 + 2 = 4

2 x 2 = 4

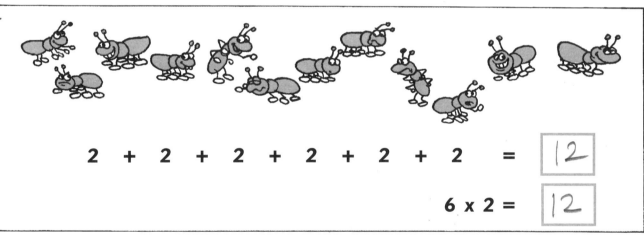

2 + 2 + 2 + 2 + 2 + 2 = 12

6 x 2 = 12

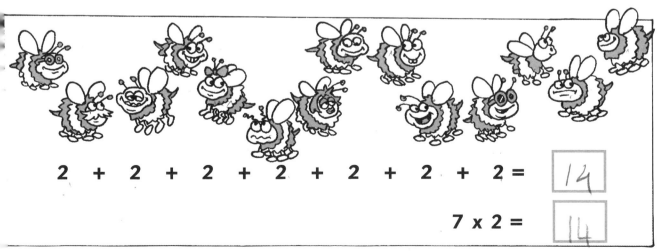

2 + 2 + 2 + 2 + 2 + 2 + 2 = 14

7 x 2 = 14

Adding lots of numbers

Dave is trying to finish his work quickly so he can go out to play.

5 + 5 + 5 = 15 can be written as

3 x 5 = 15

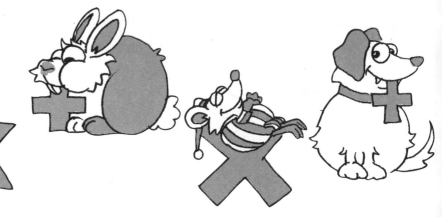

► This activity gives your child practice with multiplication as 'repeated addition'.

► Give them buttons or counters to help with their sums.

Parents

44

8

Help Dave to write these sums the short way.

5 + 5 + 5 + 5 + 5 + 5 = 30

$6 \times 5 = 30$

5 + 5 + 5 + 5 = 20

$4 \times 5 = 20$

10 + 10 + 10 + 10 + 10 + 10 = 60

$6 \times 10 = 60$

10 + 10 + 10 + 10 = 40

$4 \times 10 = 40$

2 + 2 + 2 + 2 + 2 + 2 + 2 = 14

$7 \times 2 = 14$

2 + 2 + 2 + 2 = 8

$4 \times 2 = 8$

5   8

Remember, the 'x' sign makes long addition sums shorter.

Fruity groups

Complete these sums.

$$2 \times 3 = 6$$

$$2 \times 4 = 8$$

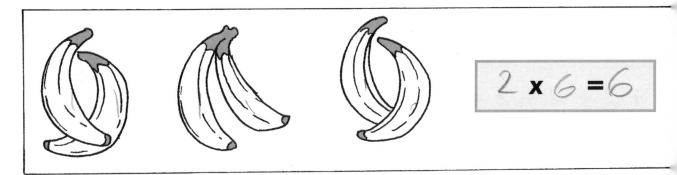

$$2 \times 6 = 6$$

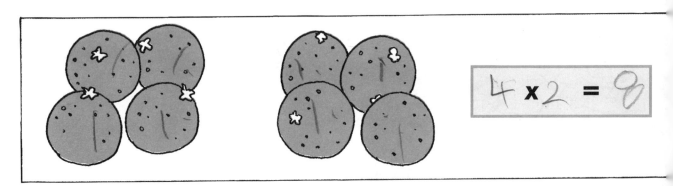

$$4 \times 2 = 8$$

This activity will help your child to 'see' multiplication as 'sets of' objects.

Encourage them to write the sums in the boxes.

3 x 3 = 9

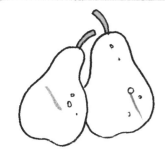 

2 x 2 = 4

2 x 4 = 8

3 x 1 = 3

Two twins

2 **sandwiches**

Perran and Carenza are twins. Their mum Clare has to buy double of everything for their lunchboxes. Can you help her work out what she needs? Write the amounts in the border.

1 **apples**

4 **chocolate fingers**

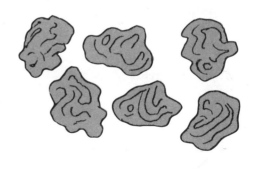

3 **raisins**

This activity introduces your child to the idea of 'doubling' numbers.

Make sure they write the answers in the boxes.

44

Doubling is when you times something by 2.

3 **crackers**

5 **grapes**

Now double these numbers:

3 | 6   5 | 10   2 | 4   4 | 8

6 | 12   1 | 2   7 | 14   10 | 20

11

Multiplication magic

Work out these multiplication calculations.

1. 2 x 2 = 4

2. 4 x 2 = 8

3. 6 x 2 = 12

4. 2 x 3 = 6

5. 3 x 3 = 9

6. 2 x 1 = 2

7. 3 x 1 = 3

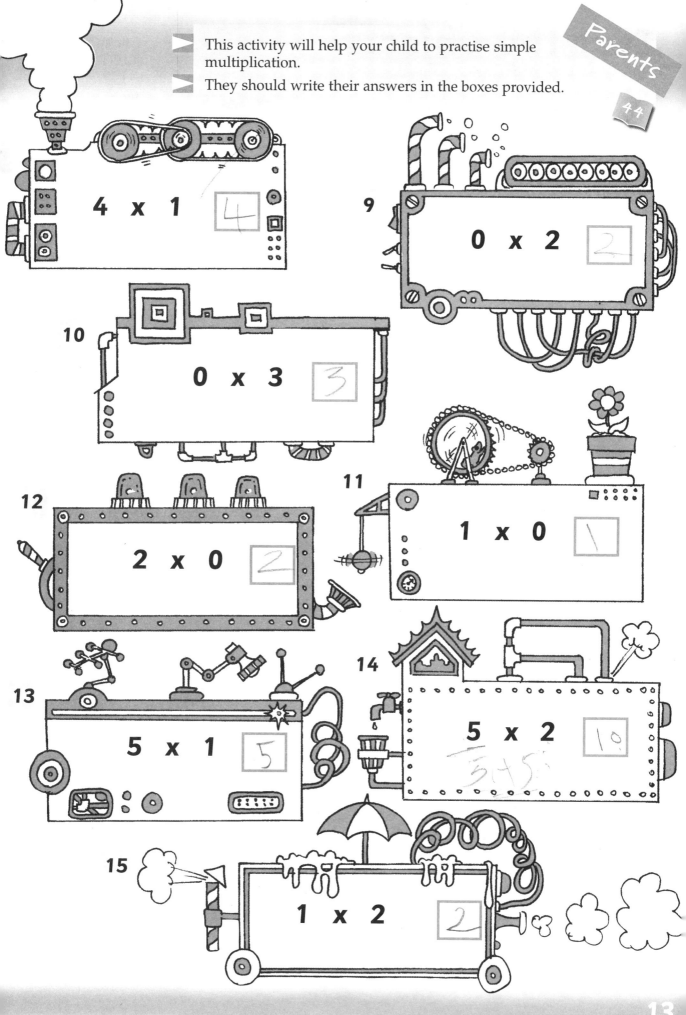

This activity will help your child to practise simple multiplication.

They should write their answers in the boxes provided.

4 x 1 = 4

9   0 x 2 = 2

10   0 x 3 = 3

12   2 x 0 = 2

11   1 x 0 = 1

13   5 x 1 = 5

14   5 x 2 = 10

15   1 x 2 = 2

Sort the objects

Katy has 12 buttons and she has drawn them in two ways like this:

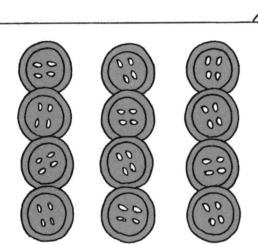

3 sets of 4

4 sets of 3

Draw 15 buttons as:

5 sets of 3

3 sets of 5

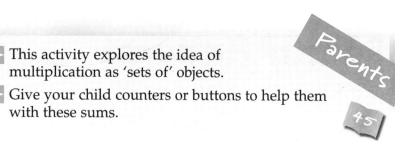

▶ This activity explores the idea of multiplication as 'sets of' objects.

▶ Give your child counters or buttons to help them with these sums.

Parents

45

Draw 10 flowers as:

2 sets of 5   **5 sets of 2**

Draw 8 tadpoles as:

4 sets of 2   **2 sets of 4**

Draw 6 stars as:

2 sets of 3   **3 sets of 2**

Funny fingers!

Look at these children waving.

3 **children are waving so there are** 15 **fingers moving.**

5 **children are answering questions so**
there are 25 **fingers moving.**

2 **children are stroking cats so there are** 10 **fingers**
moving.

5   **10**   **15**   **20**   **25**

This activity will help your child to practise the 5 times table.

Remind them to count all five fingers on each hand, even if they can't see them all.

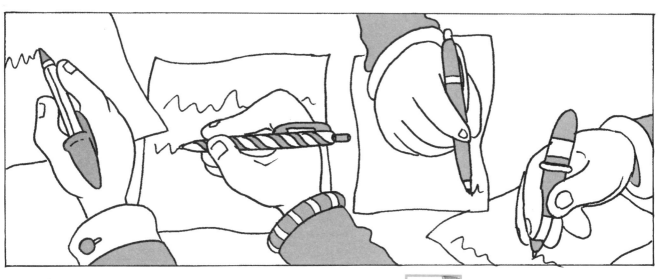

4 children are writing so there are fingers moving.

6 children are brushing their teeth so there are 30 fingers moving.

30　　**35**　　**40**　　**45**　　**50**

17

Split the chocolate

A bar of Scrumdelicious Chocolate has 10 squares.

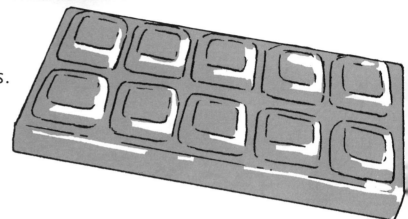

How many squares are there in:

1

3 bars

 squares

2

5 bars

 squares

3

2 bars

squares

This activity will help your child to practise the 10 times table.

Give your child counters or pasta shells to help them with their sums.

Parents

45

4

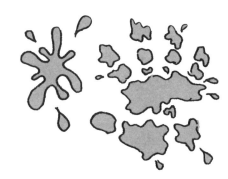

squares

4 bars

5

squares

6 bars

6

squares

8 bars

7

squares

9 bars

Looking for patterns

Read these times tables aloud.
Can you remember them without looking?

2x table

0   2   4   6   8   10

2 x 1 = 2

5x table

0   5   10   15   20

10x table

0   10   20   30   40   50

This activity will reinforce your child's knowledge of the 2, 5 and 10 times tables.

Help them to colour in the answers to learn the patterns.

12 14 16 18 20

5 30 35 40 45 50

60 70 80 90 100

Number stories

Write the answers to these multiplication
number stories.

3 crabs had 2 bits of seaweed each. How many bits of
seaweed were there altogether?

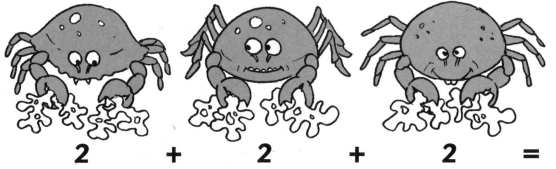

2 + 2 + 2 = 6

4 bears had 3 pots of honey each. How many pots of
honey were there altogether?

3 + 3 + 3 + 3 =

2 little girls had 5 bracelets each. How many bracelets
were there altogether?

5 + 5 =

This activity will help your child to relate multiplication to real life.

Help your child to make up 'number stories' of their own so they become familiar with multiplication and division.

5 dogs had 2 bones each. How many bones were there altogether?

2 + **2** + **2** + **2** + **2** = 10

6 mice had 2 pieces of cheese each. How many pieces of cheese were there altogether?

2 + **2** + **2** + **2** + **2** + **2** = 12

2 little boys had 5 strawberries each. How many strawberries were there altogether?

5 + **5** = 10

23

Share it out

Suzy and Ian have 20 sweets. Share them equally
into their bags by drawing them.
How many do they have each?

This activity introduces division as sharing.

Give your child real sweets to 'share' to help them with their sums.

Parents

46

Harvey is sharing his bag of sweets with Grant. Share the sweets equally into their bowls by drawing them. How many do they have each?

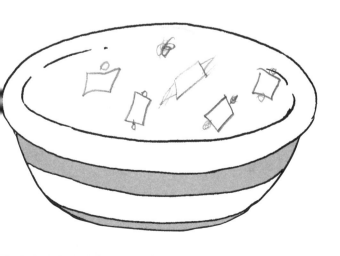

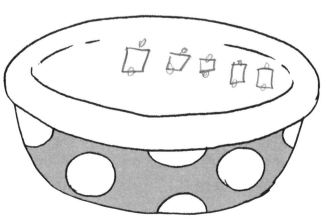

Animal sharing

There are 6 cats and 12 fish.
How many fish are there for each cat?

There are $\boxed{2}$ **fish for each cat.**

There are 4 rabbits and 12 carrots.
How many carrots are there for each rabbit?

There are $\boxed{3}$ **carrots for each rabbit.**

There are 3 dogs and 9 bones.
How many bones are there for each dog?

There are $\boxed{3}$ **bones for each dog.**

This activity shows how to share a large number of objects between a smaller number.

Give your child counters, beads or buttons to support their work.

There are 2 guinea pigs and 8 lettuce leaves.
How many leaves are there for each guinea pig?

There are leaves for each guinea pig.

There are 5 gerbils and 15 sunflower seeds.
How many seeds are there for each gerbil?

There are seeds for each gerbil.

There are 7 fish and 14 fish flakes.
How many flakes are there for each fish?

There are flakes for each fish.

27

Karim's birthday!

It is Karim's birthday. Help him to make 6 party bags by sharing out the toys and sweets.

Bethany

Eleanor

Adam

There are ☐ 🍬 each.

There are ☐ 🍭 each.

This activity gives your child practice sharing larger numbers.

Help them to draw the sweets and pencils on the bags and point out that this sharing is called division.

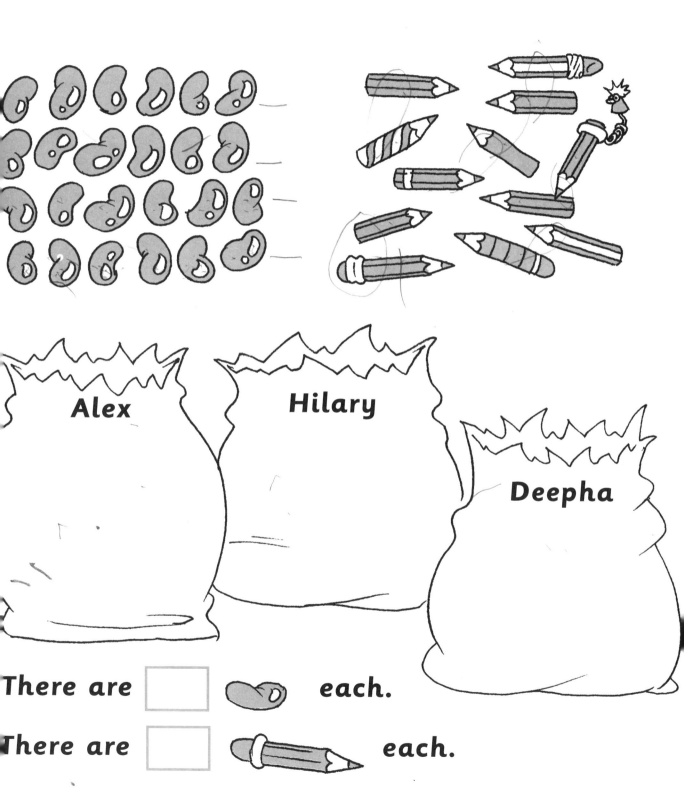

Alex

Hilary

Deepha

There are ☐ 🫘 each.

There are ☐ ✏️ each.

29

Dominic's 'double-it' spell

Dominic is using a spell to double these numbers. Write in his answers.

This activity introduces your child to doubling numbers up to 10.

Explain that 'doubling' is the same as 'times by 2'.

Parents

46

6

7

3

10

9

8

31

Break them up

There are 5 flowers and 10 caterpillars.
Share the caterpillars out equally. How many
caterpillars will there be on each flower?
Join them with a line.

There are 6 bricks and 24 snails. Share the snails out equally.
How many snails will there be on each brick?
Join them with a line.

Professor Doom's halving machine

Oh no! Wicked Professor Doom has invented a machine that halves all the numbers in the world. Write the halves of each of the numbers.

20 ☐

4 | 4

6 ☐

16 ☐

12 ☐

Parents

This activity will show your child that halving is the same as dividing by 2.

Provide dried pasta in even numbers to help them 'see' halving by 2.

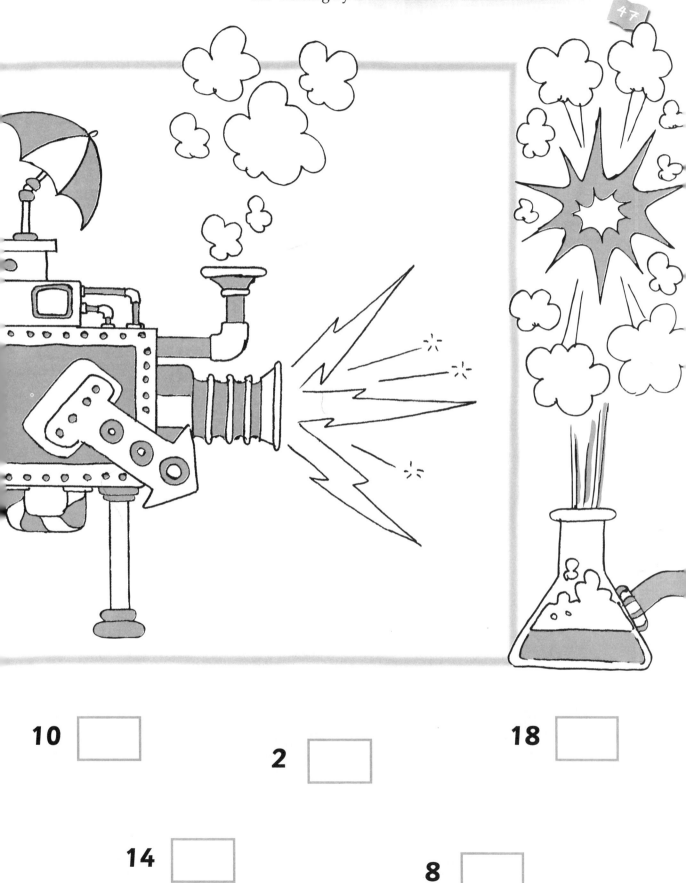

10 ▢

2 ▢

18 ▢

14 ▢

8 ▢

Snaky sequences

Remember, division 'undoes' multiplication by reversing the process.

Fill in the missing numbers.

1 $6 \times 2 = 12$ $12 \div 2 = 6$

2 $3 \times 2 = 6$ $6 \div 2 = 3$

3 $5 \times 2 = 10$ $10 \div 2 = \boxed{}$

4 $8 \times 2 = 16$ $16 \div 2 = \boxed{}$

5 $9 \times 2 = 18$ $18 \div 2 = \boxed{}$

6 $7 \times 2 = 14$ $14 \div 2 = \square$

7 $10 \times 2 = 20$ $20 \div 2 = \square$

8 $2 \times 2 = 4$ $4 \div 2 = \square$

9 $4 \times 2 = 8$ $8 \div 2 = \square$

10 $1 \times 2 = 2$ $2 \div 2 = \square$

What do you notice about each calculation pair?

Calculation chains

Look at these chains.
Fill in the missing numbers.

1 x 5 = 5   5 ÷ 5 = 1

1 x 10 = 10   10 ÷ 10 = 1

2 x 5 = 10   10 ÷ 5 = 2

2 x 10 = 20   20 ÷ 10 = 2

3 x 5 = 15   15 ÷ 5 = 3

3 x 10 = 30   30 ÷ 10 = 3

This activity will help your child to practise the relationship between x and ÷.

Point out that each set of calculations has the same numbers.

Parents

47

$5 \times 1 = 5$

$5 \div 1 = \boxed{}$

$10 \times \boxed{} = 10$

$10 \div \boxed{} = 10$

$5 \times 2 = \boxed{}$

$10 \div \boxed{} = 5$

$10 \times 2 = \boxed{}$

$20 \div 2 = \boxed{}$

$5 \times \boxed{} = 15$

$15 \div 3 = \boxed{}$

$10 \times 3 = \boxed{}$

$30 \div \boxed{} = \boxed{}$

What do you notice about each chain?

39

At the grocer's

Gary, Maggie, Simon and Rosie have some money to spend. How much fruit do they buy?

grapes 10p

raspberries 2p

bananas 5p

Gary has 20p.

How many apples can he buy?

4

Maggie has 30p.

How many strawberries can she buy?

10

apples
★ 5p ★

strawberries
3p

oranges
8p

Simon has 10p.

How many raspberries can he buy?

5

Rosie has 20p.

How many bananas can she buy?

4

Feed the rabbits

Join each carrot calculation to its matching rabbit answer.

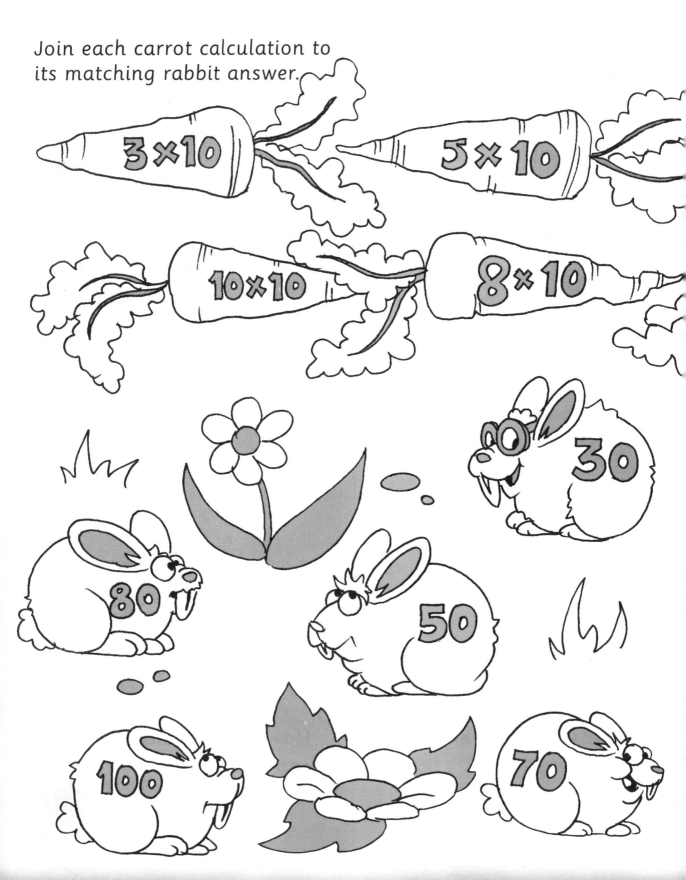

This activity offers further practice using the 10x table.

Make sure your child joins the 'calculation carrots' to their correct 'answer rabbits'.

Further activities

Extend this activity by laying out sets of objects, for instance, 3 sets of 2 cups. Say to your child 'Look, here are 2 + 2 + 2 cups. That's the same as 3 times 2. How many cups do I have?'

Repeat with other sets.

Answers: 10, 6, 8, 4, 12, 14.

This activity may be developed by writing out strings of additions, such as 2 + 2 + 2 + 2, and asking your child to write them out in the 'short way' as 4 x 2.

Answers: 6 x 5 = 30, 4 x 5 = 20, 6 x 10 = 60, 4 x 10 = 40, 7 x 2 = 14, 4 x 2 = 8.

Use sets of real objects to broaden your child's understanding of maths as sets of objects. Lay out, for example, 2 sets of 2 teddies. Encourage your child to write the sum that would record the sets, such as 2 x 2 = 4. Repeat with other sets.

Answers: 2 x 4 = 8, 3 x 2 = 6, 2 x 4 = 8, 3 x 3 = 9, 2 x 2 = 4, 4 x 2 = 8, 3 x 1 = 3.

'Play' with real food to extend 'doubling' by laying out quantities of fruit, biscuits or sweets and inviting your child to match the quantities. Point out that this is the same as doubling them.

Answers: Mum needs 4 sandwiches, 2 apples, 8 chocolate fingers, 12 raisins, 6 crackers and 10 grapes. The double numbers are 3 = 6, 5 = 10, 2 = 4, 4 = 8, 6 = 12, 1 = 2, 7 = 14, 10 = 20.

Decorate a box lid to look like a machine using foil and coloured paper stuck on shapes. Make a set of 0–20 cards. Give your child a number card, say 3, and ask them to find the answer to a sum, such as 2 x 3. They should then choose the '6' card from the box.

Answers: 2. 8, 3. 12, 4. 6, 5. 9, 6. 2, 7. 3, 8. 4, 9. 0, 10. 0, 11. 0, 12. 0, 13. 5, 14. 10, 15. 2.

Lay out objects such as buttons, beads or shells in sets, perhaps in 4 lines of 2. Then lay out 2 lines of 4. Say 'This is 4 sets of 2 and this is 2 sets of 4. How many buttons are there in each set?' Show them that 4 sets of 2 is the same as 2 sets of 4.

Count on in fives as you hold up each hand, that is, hold up one hand and say '5' then the second and say '10'. Teach your child to count in fives to 50, if possible. Don't be surprised if your child does not know that a hand has five fingers – many do not yet understand this.

Answers: Make sure your child counts all the fingers, not just the prominent ones. 15, 25, 10, 20, 30 fingers.

To broaden this activity, make card representations of 'Scrumdelicious Chocolate'. Cut small cards and rule them into 10 squares. Lay a number of cards out and ask your child to tell you how many squares there are.

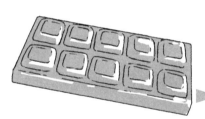

Repeat with other number of cards.

Answers: 1. 30, 2. 50, 3. 20, 4. 40, 5. 60, 6. 80, 7. 90.

Make large number strips by ruling three strips of card into 11 segments. Write 0–20 (counting in twos), 0–50 (counting in fives) 0–100 (counting in tens). Help your child to colour them in bright colours. Then display them where your child will become familiar with the sequences.

Count them together often. Write the sequence 0–20, counting in twos, vertically down the page and look for patterns with your child (0, 2, 4, 6, 8 repeats). Write the sequence 0–50, counting in fives, vertically downwards and look for patterns (0, 5 repeats). Point out that counting in tens always ends in 0.

Encourage your child to make up scenarios for teddies, dolls, pets or family members to practise this skill of repeated addition.

Answers: 12 pots of honey, 10 bracelets, 10 bones, 12 pieces of cheese, 10 strawberries.

Further activities

24-25

▶ Practise sharing real sweets into 2 sets. Encourage your child to estimate how many sweets each person will receive.

▶ *Answers: Suzy and Ian have 10 sweets each. Harvey and Grant have 5 sweets each.*

26-27

▶ Sit toys in a circle and ask your child to share out cups, spoons and pasta shells. Encourage them to estimate how many items each toy will receive.

▶ *Answers: 2 fish each, 3 carrots, 3 bones, 4 leaves, 3 sunflower seeds, 2 fish flakes.*

28-29

▶ Encourage your child to make up pretend 'party bags' for their toys, ensuring that each toy gets the same set of items.

▶ *Answers: 18 sweets = 3 each,*
6 lollies = 1 each,
24 jellybeans = 4 each,
12 pencils = 2 each.

30-31

▶ Practise 'doubling' numbers with a set of 1–10 number cards, and another set numbered 1–20. Offer your child a card from the first set, and ask them to

find the corresponding 'double' card from the second set. Repeat as often as you can.

▶ *Answers: doubles: 1 = 2, 4 = 8, 2 = 4, 5 = 10, 6 = 12, 7 = 14, 3 = 6, 10 = 20, 9 = 18, 8 = 16.*

32-33

▶ Use every opportunity to extend your child's experience of 'sharing', at the shops and at mealtimes.

▶ *Answers: There are 2 caterpillars on each flower, there are 4 snails on each brick.*

Use the cards made for the previous activity 'backwards', that is to find the corresponding 'half'. Take care to give your child only even number cards as their 'first set'.

Answers: halves: 4 = 2, 20 = 10, 16 = 8, 6 = 3, 12 = 6, 10 = 5, 14 = 7, 2 = 1, 8 = 4, 18 = 9.

To extend this activity, write out a multiplication sum and help your child to find the corresponding division.

Answers: 3. 10 ÷ 2 = 5, 4. 16 ÷ 2 = 8, 5. 18 ÷ 2 = 9, 6. 14 ÷ 2 = 7, 7. 20 ÷ 2 = 10, 8. 4 ÷ 2 = 2, 9. 8 ÷ 2 = 4, 10. 2 ÷ 2 = 1.

This is a difficult activity that will require lots of practice. Read the sums to your child and encourage them to find the missing number. Extend this with other sets of numbers that you write on paper.

Answers: 1 x 5 = 5, 5 ÷ 5 = 1, 5 x 1 = 5, 5 ÷ 1 = 5 1 x 10 = 10, 10 ÷ 10 = 1, 10 x 1 = 10, 10 ÷ 1 = 10 2 x 5 = 10, 10 ÷ 5 = 2, 5 x 2 = 10, 10 ÷ 2 = 5 2 x 10 = 20, 20 ÷ 10 = 2, 10 x 2 = 20, 20 ÷ 2 = 10 3 x 5 = 15, 15 ÷ 5 = 3, 5 x 3 = 15, 15 ÷ 3 = 5 3 x 10 = 30, 30 ÷ 10 = 3, 10 x 3 = 30, 30 ÷ 3 = 10.

Broaden this activity by using real objects and money. Label toys with 'prices' and ask your child how many 2p toys they could buy with 10p, how many 5p toys can they buy with 50p, and so on.

Answers: Gary buys 4 apples, Maggie buys 10 strawberries, Simon buys 5 raspberries, Rosie buys 4 bananas.

This activity offers your child further practice using the 10 times table. Extend this by making a set of cards 10–100 for them to sequence. You could also make a 0–100 number line and ask your child to colour in the multiples of 10.

Answers: 80 = 8 x 10, 100 = 10 x 10, 30 = 3 x 10, 50 = 5 x 10, 70 = 7 x 10, 90 = 9 x 10, 60 = 6 x 10, 40 = 4 x 10, 20 = 2 x 10.

Celebration!

I can multiply by 2.

I know doubling is the same as times 2.

I know halving is the same as dividing by 2.